A GAY HISTORY
OF AUSSIE
BLOKES

I0437657

DOWN
UNDER
GAY
BLOKES

ROBBIE GROWLR

BEST
SELLER

F or as long as there have been people on the great continent now known as Australia, there have been diverse expressions of gender and sexuality. And yet, it wasn't until the arrival of the Europeans that these expressions began to be categorized and stigmatized.

As the sails of Captain Cook's ship crested the horizon, there was no way for the Indigenous people to know what lay in store for their many diverse cultures and ways of life. The Aboriginal communities had a rich and nuanced understanding of gender and sexuality, with many tribes recognizing and accepting what would later be categorized under the umbrella of non-heteronormative identities.

The Europeans, however, arrived with very different notions. The Puritanical sexual mores of Victorian England couldn't have been more at odds with the local customs. With this cultural clash, began the erasure and vilification of non-heteronormative identities.

In the early colonial period, homosexuality was considered a criminal act, a sin, or a mental disorder. By the 19th century, 'buggery' was a capital crime in New South Wales, and it would take more than a hundred years for laws against homosexuality to be entirely abolished.

The infamous 'Tasmanian case' marked a turning point in the early 20th century. A Tasmanian man, known in the media only as 'James', was arrested and charged with 'gross indecency' in 1954. He pleaded guilty and was given a prison sentence. The shocking injustice of the case rallied public sympathy, and a groundswell of support began to grow.

"I felt like an animal, a criminal," James' words echo in the annals of

Australia's gay history. His ordeal and courage became a catalyst for change, galvanizing the nascent gay rights movement.

By the 1970s, change was on the horizon. Inspired by the Stonewall riots in the United States and the sexual revolution globally, Australian gay rights activists began to rally, with organizations like Campaign Against Moral Persecution (CAMP) pioneering the charge.

A group of CAMP members, including foundational figures Sue Wills and John Ware, banded together to create Australia's first gay and lesbian newspaper, 'Camp Ink.' It became an invaluable source of information and community, particularly for those isolated due to societal prejudice.

Indeed, as Ware himself famously said, "we weren't just making a newspaper; we were building a community."

Throughout the 1970s and 1980s, brave individuals stood up and fought for their rights, marching, protesting, and lobbying for change. By 1997, Tasmania, the last holdout, had decriminalized homosexuality, marking a significant legal milestone.

While legislative progress was hard-won, societal attitudes shifted more slowly. The stigma associated with homosexuality was deeply entrenched, and discrimination was widespread. But through it all, the resilient LGBTQIA+ community stood firm, and their stories became the fabric of Australia's rich and complex gay history. The trail they blazed still shines brightly, a beacon of hope for future generations.

But this is not just a tale of adversity; it's also a story of joy, of community, and of love. It's a story that continues to evolve and unfold to this day, weaving a rich tapestry of diversity that is as varied and vibrant as the land itself. As we delve deeper into Australia's gay history, let us remember the resilience, courage, and spirit of those who dared to be true to themselves, shaping Australia into the diverse and accepting country it aspires to be today.

The sun was setting over Sydney Harbour on a September evening in 1970 when a small group gathered at a house in Balmain. This unassuming meeting would go on to be recognised as the humble inception of an influential force for change in Australia - the Campaign Against Moral Persecution, commonly known as CAMP Inc.

In the headlines the next year, CAMP Inc. announced its arrival to the nation. The Sydney Morning Herald printed an interview with the organization's founders, John Ware and Christabel Poll. The couple unapologetically acknowledged their homosexuality on national media, a brave step in the face of existing prejudices.

"The homosexual is a very second-class citizen... the law says you're a criminal," Ware told the Herald.

However, this was only the tip of the iceberg. CAMP Inc.'s work expanded to include counseling, legal advice, and a 'meet the people' program where members would speak to university students and social groups to increase awareness about homosexuality and challenge stereotypes.

Among the publications CAMP Inc. put out, the newsletter 'Camp Ink' holds a special place. A vehicle for advocacy, education, and community-building, it became an invaluable lifeline for those isolated due to their sexuality.

"We were creating something that was quite new in Australia... For the first time, there was a radical critique of how society handled homosexuality," said Sue Wills, one of the original staff members of 'Camp Ink,' in a later interview.

The 70s marked not only the rise of advocacy groups but also a public coming out of the Australian gay community. The Sydney Gay and Lesbian Mardi Gras, originally planned as a street demonstration in 1978, faced police violence and public backlash. Despite this, the event marked a significant turning point in Australian gay rights history.

"For those of us who were there, the night was a moment of liberation... At last, we were standing up publicly and collectively to challenge the system," said Lance Gowland, one of the original 78ers - participants in the inaugural Mardi Gras.

Around the same time, various other organizations sprouted up across Australia. These included Phone-A-Friend (later renamed to Gay and Lesbian Counselling Service) in 1973, and Acceptance - a supportive group for gay Catholics - in 1972.

In Victoria, the Homosexual Law Reform Coalition worked tirelessly on legislative reform. "The law reform campaign is not just about homosexuality, but it is about the rights of all minority groups," affirmed Jamie Gardiner, a leading figure of the Coalition, in an interview with The Age.

While these early years of the gay rights movement were marred by prejudice, violence, and legislative hurdles, they also witnessed an unyielding resilience. Groups and individuals, bonded by a shared cause, emerged from the shadows to challenge societal norms. Through a shared understanding of their common struggle and a vision for a fairer future, they laid the groundwork for future victories and kindled a flame that continues to burn brightly.

As we examine these events, it is important to remember these brave pioneers who dared to challenge the status quo. Their courage and conviction propelled the early gay rights movement, pushing Australian society to confront its prejudices and change for the better.

With the 20th century in full swing, Australian society's views on homosexuality were gradually shifting. While the preceding decades were characterized by repression and stigma, the latter part of the century saw determined strides towards acceptance and equality. Among these victories, the decriminalization of homosexuality was a landmark achievement.

Decriminalization didn't occur overnight, nor was it handed down without a fight. It was the result of years of relentless advocacy, dogged determination, and a society increasingly questioning the status quo.

South Australia led the charge in 1975 when Don Dunstan's government successfully passed the Criminal Law (Sexual Offences) Act 1975, repealing the antiquated sodomy laws. "The law has no place in the bedrooms of consenting adults," Dunstan famously declared during the legislation debate.

While South Australia paved the way, other states were slower to follow suit. It was not until 1980 that Victoria passed the Crimes (Sexual Offences) Act, which decriminalized homosexual acts between consenting adults. "Homosexuality is not a sickness, not a crime, and not immoral," remarked then Attorney-General Haddon Storey.

New South Wales, home to the vibrant Sydney gay and lesbian scene, decriminalized homosexuality in 1984, as did the Australian Capital Territory. "The law's domain is not morality," stated then New South Wales Premier Neville Wran, "it is to maintain public order and decency, to protect the citizen from what is injurious or offensive, and to provide sufficient safeguards against exploitation and corruption of others."

The last Australian state to decriminalize homosexuality was Tasmania, in 1997, after a prolonged and hard-fought battle led by activists such as Rodney Croome. "When I was a teenager, I realised that according to the law of my state, I was a criminal. It was a shocking realisation, and it made me feel very isolated. I knew then that something had to change," Croome recalled in a 1997 interview.

The decriminalization of homosexuality was not just a triumph for gay men, but a victory for human rights and equality. Nevertheless, while these changes to the criminal codes removed the worst of the legal discrimination, social prejudice remained. Violence, social ostracism, and discrimination were still everyday realities for many LGBTQIA+ individuals.

Despite the continued challenges, this pivotal moment in history marked a seismic shift in society's understanding and acceptance of homosexuality. Looking back on this era, it is crucial to remember the immense courage and tireless efforts of countless individuals and advocacy groups. They defied the status quo, challenged ingrained prejudice, and brought about transformative change.

The echoes of their voices resound through history, reminding us of the progress made, and the work still to be done. Their fight was not just for legal acceptance but for societal change, for the right to love freely, to exist without fear, and to be treated with dignity and respect. As we reflect on these important milestones, we celebrate their resilience, their bravery, and their indomitable spirit.

In the swirling social movements of the late 20th century, a new sense of identity and community was emerging among gay men and women in Australia. From the clandestine bars of Sydney's King Cross to the bohemian laneways of Melbourne's Carlton, enclaves of acceptance and self-expression began to form, setting the stage for what would eventually become Australia's vibrant gay neighbourhoods.

Nestled in the heart of Sydney, Darlinghurst and its famed Oxford Street became the beating heart of the city's gay scene. Home to the symbolic Sydney Gay and Lesbian Mardi Gras parade, this area became a haven for the LGBTQIA+ community. One of the area's best-known establishments, the Oxford Hotel, opened its doors in the 1980s and quickly became a popular venue for gay men.

"Oxford Street was more than just a place, it was a feeling of belonging, an acceptance of who you are without judgment," reminisced David Wilkins, a regular at the Oxford Hotel.

In Melbourne, the gay scene took a more bohemian bent, emerging amidst the coffee houses and Italian trattorias of Carlton. While less flashy than Sydney's scene, Melbourne's gay community prided itself on its intellectual and artistic flair. The Val's Coffee Lounge, a bohemian café in the heart of Carlton, served as a key meeting place for Melbourne's gay and lesbian community in the 1960s and 70s.

"Not only could we be ourselves at Val's, but we could also meet others like us. It was an extraordinary place of acceptance during a time of widespread prejudice," said Maria Pallotta-Chiarolli, a prominent LGBTQIA+ researcher.

Over in Brisbane, the Fortitude Valley was fast becoming the city's epicentre of gay culture. In the late 1980s, the Sportsman Hotel, affectionately known as 'Sporties', emerged as a popular spot for Brisbane's gay community.

"I remember walking into Sporties for the first time and feeling like I had finally found my tribe," former patron Rob Collins recalled. "There was a sense of community there that I had never experienced before."

Meanwhile, Adelaide's gay scene coalesced around the Colonel Light Hotel, or the 'Col Light' as locals called it. While Adelaide was slower than Sydney or Melbourne in developing visible gay spaces, the 'Col Light' became the city's first openly gay venue in the early 1970s.

"Going to the 'Col Light' was a statement, a public declaration of who you were," said former patron Simon Hunt, later known as Pauline Pantsdown, a political satirist. "It wasn't always easy, but there was a sense of solidarity and mutual support that was incredibly empowering."

The creation of these gay neighbourhoods across Australia signified more than just the establishment of safe spaces for socialisation and support. They were symbols of resilience and visibility in the face of societal prejudice, they represented a tangible manifestation of community identity and pride. These neighbourhoods not only fostered a sense of belonging among those who felt outcast from mainstream society but also played a crucial role in the broader fight for LGBTQIA+ rights and acceptance.

Whether it was the vibrant parades of Sydney's Oxford Street, the bohemian cafes of Melbourne's Carlton, or the camaraderie of Brisbane's 'Sporties,' these spaces held the echoes of countless stories of love, joy, struggle, and triumph. They stand as powerful testaments to the enduring spirit of the LGBTQIA+ community, monuments to a shared history that continues to shape Australia's cultural landscape.

In contrast to the inspiring community-building and progress in gay rights, the landscape of homophobia in Australia presented a different, darker perspective on the history of gay men in the nation. From the political arena to the streets, homophobia was a formidable hurdle that the LGBTQIA+ community faced in their fight for acceptance and equality.

The socio-political sphere was a significant platform for the perpetuation of homophobia. Political resistance to LGBTQIA+ rights took shape in various forms, from opposition to law reforms, derogatory comments by public figures, and policies that marginalised the community.

In 1977, former New South Wales Premier Robert Askin infamously described homosexuality as "a subject I do not discuss." This sentiment was indicative of the widespread political reluctance to address issues of sexual orientation and rights.

Such political resistance was not without its consequences. Dr. Jo Harrison, a prominent researcher of older LGBTQIA+ Australians, highlighted that, "the lack of political will to address issues concerning sexual orientation has severe implications. It reinforces the marginalisation of the gay community, contributes to continued discrimination, and creates a hostile environment."

The societal impact of homophobia was equally, if not more, distressing. According to a national survey conducted by the Australian Human Rights Commission in 2003, 74% of respondents had experienced some form of verbal abuse due to their sexual orientation, while 26% reported physical assault.

"These statistics are a startling reminder of the extent of homophobia in our society," said then Human Rights Commissioner, Sev Ozdowski. "Such prejudice not only affects individuals but also hampers the progress of our society as a whole."

In response to this hostile environment, several community initiatives were undertaken to combat homophobia. Groups such as the Anti-Violence Project of Victoria began to provide support for victims and work towards the prevention of hate crimes.

Education became a crucial tool to counteract the ignorance and fear that often underlay homophobia. Programs like Safe Schools Coalition Australia, launched in 2014, aimed to create safer, inclusive environments in schools for students of diverse sexual orientations.

"Homophobia is born out of ignorance," said Roz Ward, one of the architects of the Safe Schools program. "Education can be the antidote to that ignorance, providing a means to understanding, acceptance, and ultimately, equality."

Despite the institutional and societal barriers that homophobia presented, the LGBTQIA+ community's resilience in the face of such adversity remained unyielding. They continued their struggle for acceptance, inclusion, and equality, refusing to be silenced by hate or fear.

Homophobia's mark on Australia's gay history cannot be overlooked or understated. It stands as a somber testament to the trials and tribulations the LGBTQIA+ community has endured. However, it also highlights their incredible fortitude and perseverance in the face of adversity, a testament to their enduring fight for acceptance and equality.

At the intersection of art and activism, cinema holds a powerful place in society. Within its frames, it captures the ethos of an era, reflects societal norms, and can also challenge them. In Australia, queer cinema, defined as cinema that represents LGBTQIA+ themes and characters, has been instrumental in promoting visibility and influencing cultural attitudes towards homosexuality.

Early Australian cinema rarely portrayed gay characters, and when they did appear, they were often depicted in a stereotypical or derogatory light. The 1978 film, 'The Night, The Prowler,' for instance, used a gay character as comic relief, a representation that was less than favourable. This trend was indicative of the wider societal attitudes towards homosexuality during that time.

The 1980s saw a shift in queer representation, and Australian cinema began to explore more nuanced depictions of gay characters. One of the most notable examples is the 1982 film 'Night Out.' "Night Out was groundbreaking," recalled its director, Lawrence Johnston. "We were unapologetically exploring gay male sexuality, something that hadn't been done before in Australian cinema."

The '90s marked a new era of representation with films like 'The Adventures of Priscilla, Queen of the Desert' (1994), an iconic Australian film that brought drag culture into mainstream consciousness. "Priscilla was a celebration of drag culture and queerness," said star Terence Stamp. "It was bold, unafraid, and it resonated with people, gay and straight alike."

In the new millennium, 'Holding the Man' (2015), based on Timothy Conigrave's memoir, presented a raw and moving story of a gay couple navigating their relationship amid societal prejudice and the AIDS crisis. The film was lauded for its poignant depiction of the complexities and struggles faced by gay men during the 1980s and 90s. "Our aim was to tell a universal love story that just happened to be between two men," said director Neil Armfield.

Today, queer cinema in Australia continues to evolve, becoming ever more diverse in its representation of LGBTQIA+ characters and stories. Films such as 'Ellie & Abbie (& Ellie's Dead Aunt)' (2020) not only depict same-sex relationships but also tackle other aspects of the LGBTQIA+ experience, such as coming out.

"Ellie & Abbie was about showing that gay stories don't always have to be about suffering. They can be about joy, love, and the mundane everyday experiences," said writer-director Monica Zanetti.

From sparse and stereotypical depictions to nuanced and diverse portrayals, the journey of queer cinema in Australia mirrors the evolution of societal attitudes towards homosexuality. It is a reflection of the times, a testament to the changes in perception, and a powerful tool for visibility and representation. In the words of filmmaker Stephan Elliott, "Cinema has the power to change minds, and queer cinema has been doing just that."

The relationships between gay men and straight men in Australia have often been a study in contrasts, revealing nuances in societal attitudes, perceptions, and individual interactions. In the past, such friendships were often complicated by societal prejudices and stereotypes. Yet, with the evolution of societal attitudes, the dynamic between gay men and straight men began to shift, leading to a new understanding and acceptance.

Navigating friendships between gay men and straight men was, and sometimes still is, a delicate process. Social conditioning and stereotypes have played a significant role in shaping these relationships. Gay men were often burdened with the pressure to 'pass' as straight, to avoid discomfort or misunderstanding.

Reflecting on his early years, Peter de Waal, an Australian gay rights activist, said, "There was a constant fear of being found out. Friendships were difficult to navigate, especially with straight men. There was a barrier, invisible yet palpable."

Yet, as societal attitudes towards homosexuality evolved, so did these friendships. The stigmas and misconceptions that once marred these relationships began to wane, replaced with understanding and acceptance.

"I've found that the relationships between gay and straight men have changed significantly over the years," said psychologist Dr. Timothy Sharp. "We're seeing greater acceptance, greater understanding, and ultimately, stronger friendships."

These friendships have also come to play an important role in the struggle for gay rights. Straight allies have proven instrumental in advocating for change within broader society. Their presence within the fight for equality has helped challenge and change societal attitudes towards homosexuality.

Michael Kirby, a former High Court judge and prominent gay rights advocate, highlighted the importance of these allies: "Straight men have played a significant role in the battle for equality, not as saviours but as allies. Their support and understanding have been invaluable."

One such ally is Australian former footballer and mental health advocate Wayne Schwass, who has been vocal about his support for the LGBTQIA+ community. "We need to stand up, speak out and challenge homophobia," Schwass said. "As straight men, we have a responsibility to support our LGBTQIA+ mates."

Indeed, friendships between gay men and straight men are more than personal bonds; they are bridges between different experiences and perspectives. These relationships reflect societal progression, a shift from divisiveness towards understanding and acceptance. In the words of de Waal, "It's more than just about being friends. It's about recognising our common humanity."

While progress has been made, the journey towards full acceptance continues. Each friendship, each ally, contributes to this journey, breaking down barriers, one misconception at a time.

One of the unique aspects of Australian gay culture revolves around a certain affinity for rugby league shorts, often referred to as 'footy shorts,' and swimwear known as 'speedos.' These iconic pieces of Australian sportswear have taken on a cultural life of their own within the gay community, crossing over from sporting fields and pools to become symbols of style, identity, and in some instances, even fetish.

The popularity of footy shorts and speedos among gay men could be attributed to multiple factors. Some argue that it's the aesthetic appeal of these garments – form-fitting, short, and revealing – that makes them so popular. Others point towards the cultural significance and masculine image associated with these sports-oriented items.

"Footy shorts and speedos have a certain masculine appeal," said fashion historian Roger Leong. "They're associated with athleticism, physicality, and traditional Australian ideals of masculinity, which can be particularly appealing in a gay context."

Over time, footy shorts and speedos have also evolved into a distinct fashion statement within gay subcultures. Events like Sydney's Gay and Lesbian Mardi Gras often see an abundance of attendees dressed in these sportswear items, showcasing them as a part of their personal expression and style.

Brett, a regular Mardi Gras participant, commented, "At Mardi Gras, wearing footy shorts or speedos is more than just a fashion choice. It's about expressing our identity, our community. It's about owning our sexuality and being proud of it."

The significance of footy shorts and speedos has also extended into the realm of fetish within some sections of the gay community. The combination of their physical appeal, associations with masculinity, and the voyeuristic thrill of the taboo has made these items objects of sexual desire for some individuals.

"Sportswear fetishes aren't unique to the gay community," explained sexologist Dr. Nikki Goldstein. "They're more about the associations we make – with specific clothing, specific contexts. It's not just the garment itself, but what it represents."

This cultural phenomenon is also representative of a larger shift in societal attitudes towards sexuality. The celebration and fetishization of footy shorts and speedos within the gay community signals a broader acceptance of diverse sexual expressions and identities.

In the words of Professor Dennis Altman, a pioneer in the study of sexuality and politics, "The popularisation of footy shorts and speedos is part of the larger narrative of sexual liberation and acceptance. It's a testament to how far we've come."

Whether viewed through the lens of fashion, fetish, or cultural symbolism, the popularity of rugby league shorts and speedos within Australia's gay community is a unique aspect of the country's gay history and culture. It's a trend that reflects not just personal preference, but also the evolution of societal norms, attitudes, and acceptance.

Fashion is not just about the clothes we wear; it is a reflection of who we are, how we choose to express ourselves, and the societal and cultural trends of a particular era. For gay men in Australia, fashion has long been a powerful tool for self-expression and identity, as well as a significant driving force within the 'Pink Economy.'

The 'Pink Economy,' or 'Pink Dollar,' refers to the purchasing power of the LGBTQIA+ community, with gay men forming a substantial portion of this demographic. In Australia, this Pink Economy has become increasingly influential, with businesses recognizing the potential and power of the LGBTQIA+ market.

The fashion industry, in particular, has been significantly impacted by the Pink Economy. The distinctive tastes, creative flair, and high fashion consumption of many gay men have driven trends and influenced the industry's direction. Brands have recognized the potential of this market, with many featuring inclusive advertising campaigns and products that cater to diverse tastes and identities.

Australian designer Brent Wilson stated, "The gay market is vital in the fashion industry. They are often early adopters, taste-makers. They have a strong influence on fashion trends."

Beyond consumption, gay men have also contributed immensely to the industry as fashion designers, stylists, and influencers. Their unique perspectives and creative sensibilities have enriched the fashion world, making it more vibrant and diverse. Renowned Australian designer, Alex Perry, himself a gay man, commented, "Fashion is about expressing your individuality, and who you are. Gay men have brought their own unique experiences and viewpoints to the table, adding richness to the industry."

The importance of the Pink Economy extends beyond the commercial aspect. It represents the economic influence and significance of the LGBTQIA+ community, contributing to visibility and acceptance. Furthermore, businesses catering to or acknowledging the Pink Economy indirectly support the fight against discrimination by promoting inclusivity.

Dr. Mark McLelland, a professor specializing in Gender and Sexuality Studies, highlighted the social implications of the Pink Economy. "The rise of the Pink Economy has led to greater visibility and acceptance of the LGBTQIA+

community," he said. "It's more than just economics; it's about representation and inclusion."

The Pink Economy, particularly in the fashion industry, is a testament to the changing societal norms, increasing acceptance, and the emerging power of the LGBTQIA+ community in Australia. Gay men, as significant contributors to and consumers of the fashion industry, have played an integral role in shaping the industry's landscape, contributing not only to its economic growth but also to its diversity and inclusivity.

The Sydney Gay and Lesbian Mardi Gras is more than a parade; it is a bold statement of pride, acceptance, and community. It's an annual celebration of Australia's LGBTQIA+ community that takes over Sydney's streets with an outpouring of colour, creativity, and camaraderie. Yet, its origins lie in a struggle for visibility, acceptance, and equality that continues to resonate today.

On a chilly winter night in 1978, what began as a peaceful march for gay rights descended into chaos when police intervened, leading to numerous arrests. However, this confrontation sparked a powerful response from the gay community and its allies, eventually giving birth to the Sydney Gay and Lesbian Mardi Gras.

The early Mardi Gras parades were marked by defiance and determination. Participants donned handmade costumes, bearing banners that called for equality and acceptance. The mood was palpable. As one of the original 78ers, Diane

Minnis, recalls, "We were scared, but we were also proud. We were standing up for who we were."

Since those challenging early days, the Mardi Gras has evolved into a significant event on Sydney's cultural calendar. Every year, hundreds of thousands of people flock to the city to take part in the festivities. The parade is a riot of colour and celebration, featuring elaborate floats, extravagant costumes, and participants from all walks of life.

"We have come a long way since the first Mardi Gras," says 2023 Mardi Gras co-chair, Giovanni Campolo-Arcidiaco. "It's a testament to the resilience of our community, and the support we have received from all sections of society."

Yet, the Mardi Gras is not just about celebration; it continues to be a platform for activism and advocacy. Issues such as marriage equality, transgender rights, and mental health are highlighted, reminding spectators that while much has been achieved, the fight for full equality continues.

"Mardi Gras is more than just a party," says activist Sally Rugg. "It's an opportunity to celebrate our achievements, but also to reflect on the work that still needs to be done. It's about solidarity, community, and the ongoing fight for equality."

The Sydney Gay and Lesbian Mardi Gras, born from a moment of prejudice, has become a beacon of pride, not just for Sydney, but for Australia as a whole. It is a testament to the resilience of the LGBTQIA+

community, an annual celebration of how far they've come, and a reminder of the journey that still lies ahead. As Rugg puts it, "Every Mardi Gras is both a party and a protest - a colourful, loud, and unapologetic statement of who we are."

n the realm of sports, Australia's passion for rugby is renowned. It's a sport that not only embodies strength and athleticism but also camaraderie and community. And within this broader community, gay rugby has carved out a special place, breaking barriers and challenging stereotypes along the way.

Gay rugby in Australia took its first solid step in the early 2000s with the formation of the Sydney Convicts, the country's first gay-inclusive rugby union club. Their mission was simple yet profound: to provide a space where people could enjoy rugby in an environment free from homophobia.

One of the founding members, Andrew 'Fuzz' Purchas, explained, "Our goal was never just about playing rugby. It was about changing the narrative, proving that your sexual orientation doesn't define your athletic ability."

Since the Convicts' inception, they've not only proven their prowess on the field, winning multiple Bingham

Cups (the World Championship of gay rugby), but they've also paved the way for other gay rugby clubs, such as the Melbourne Chargers and the Brisbane Hustlers. These teams have been instrumental in creating inclusive environments within the traditionally masculine domain of rugby.

These clubs' impacts go beyond the rugby field. They've helped challenge preconceived notions about homosexuality in sports, promoting inclusivity and acceptance. By just playing the sport they love, these players are confronting and dismantling stereotypes, demonstrating that being gay and being a rugby player are not mutually exclusive.

"Playing rugby and being openly gay has been an empowering

experience," said Erik Denison, a researcher and former player with the Melbourne Chargers. "It challenges the stereotypes people may have about gay men not being tough or athletic."

The Australian Rugby Union (ARU) has acknowledged the importance of such inclusive clubs. In 2014, the ARU became the first Australian sporting organization to introduce an Inclusion Policy, aimed at stamping out homophobia in the sport. This policy has been a vital step in creating a more inclusive and accepting environment within rugby.

"The policy is a commitment to our people," said ARU CEO Bill Pulver. "Rugby is a sport for all, regardless of sexuality."

Gay rugby in Australia is about more than just sportsmanship. It's a movement towards acceptance, a fight against discrimination, and a beacon for those seeking a safe space to enjoy the sport they love. As Denison rightly puts it, "We're not just playing a game. We're making a statement - that everyone is welcome in rugby, regardless of who they love."

The HIV/AIDS crisis of the 1980s and 1990s left an indelible mark on the global landscape, and Australia was no exception. The pandemic's impact was particularly profound within the gay community, where it claimed many lives and reshaped social and cultural norms.

As HIV/AIDS began to take hold, fear and misunderstanding were pervasive. Gay men, who were disproportionately affected by the disease, often faced stigma and discrimination, exacerbating the crisis. Yet, in the face of adversity, the Australian gay community rallied together, leading the charge in the country's response to HIV/AIDS.

Community-based organizations like the Victorian AIDS Council (now Thorne Harbour Health) and the AIDS Council of New South Wales (now ACON) sprang into action, raising awareness about safe sex practices and advocating for those affected by HIV/AIDS. Their efforts were crucial in stemming the tide of the epidemic and fostering a community-led response.

David Menadue, one of Australia's longest living people with HIV and a prominent advocate, remembers the early years of the crisis. "It was a terrifying time," he says. "But it also brought our community together. We looked after each other, educated each other. We did what we had to do to survive."

The HIV/AIDS crisis also triggered significant advances in Australia's public health policy. The country's response, known for its bipartisan support and early focus on harm reduction, has often been lauded as one of the most effective globally. Notably, the "Grim Reaper" campaign of the late 1980s, despite its controversial nature, succeeded in bringing the severity of the AIDS crisis to the forefront of public consciousness.

Medical research in Australia also made considerable strides. The National Centre in HIV Epidemiology and Clinical Research (now the Kirby Institute) was established in 1986, driving research into HIV epidemiology, clinical virology and treatments, which has greatly contributed to understanding and managing the disease.

Today, the legacy of the HIV/AIDS crisis remains a significant part of Australia's gay history. Advances in treatment mean that HIV is now a manageable chronic condition rather than a death sentence. Pre-Exposure Prophylaxis (PrEP), a daily medication that prevents HIV, has been a game-changer, drastically reducing new HIV infections among gay and bisexual men.

Yet, while the landscape of HIV/AIDS in Australia has changed dramatically, the memories of the crisis linger. It's a chapter in the history of the gay community that underscores the profound resilience and strength in the face of adversity. As Menadue puts it, "We came through a war. We lost a lot, but we also learned how strong we can be together."

The road to marriage equality in Australia was a journey marked by dedication, perseverance, and an unwavering belief in the principle of love for all. After years of advocacy, protest, and political debate, the momentous day arrived on December 7, 2017, when the Australian Parliament passed a law legalizing same-sex marriage. This victory was more than just a legal milestone; it marked a societal shift towards acceptance and equality.

The marriage equality movement in Australia, like its counterparts worldwide, had its roots in the larger struggle for LGBTQIA+ rights. For years, the community and its allies campaigned tirelessly, rallying for change through public demonstrations, political lobbying, and grassroots activism. Yet, it was not until the nationwide postal survey in 2017 that the push for marriage equality gained unprecedented momentum.

Despite criticisms of the postal survey, the result was

overwhelmingly in favor of change. The 'Yes' vote prevailed, with 61.6% of Australians voicing their support for marriage equality. This public endorsement paved the way for political action, culminating in the Marriage Amendment (Definition and Religious Freedoms) Act 2017, which amended the Marriage Act 1961 to allow for the marriage between two people "regardless of their sex."

For the LGBTQIA+ community, the passage of the law was met with joy, relief, and a sense of validation. "It was a moment of collective triumph," said Alex Greenwich, co-chair of Australian Marriage Equality. "It was a validation of the love and commitment that same-sex couples share, and a recognition of our equal place in Australian society."

The legalization of same-sex marriage had profound social and personal implications. For many couples, it meant they could finally formalize their commitment to each other in the eyes of the law. For the broader community, it was a definitive step towards a more inclusive society.

Ian Thorpe, Olympic swimmer and a prominent figure in the 'Yes' campaign, reflected on the significance of the moment. "This was about more than marriage," he said. "It was about acceptance, about saying to young people that it's okay to be who you are."

The journey towards marriage equality in Australia was not a smooth one, but it was a testament to the power of advocacy, the resilience of the LGBTQIA+ community, and the enduring belief in love's universality. The moment the law was passed marked not the end of the journey, but the beginning of a new era of inclusivity and acceptance Down Under. As Greenwich beautifully summed it up, "This was not just a change in law. It was a change in hearts and minds."

T hroughout Australia's history, the journey towards LGBTQIA+ rights has been shaped by the tireless efforts of numerous activists, community leaders, and organizations. These individuals and groups have played a crucial role in fighting discrimination, advocating for policy change, and pushing society towards greater acceptance and equality.

Peter de Waal and Peter Bonsall-Boone, often known as "the Peters", were early pioneers of gay activism in Australia. Their decision to publicly declare their love on national television in 1972 marked a groundbreaking moment in the country's gay rights history. Bonsall-Boone was subsequently fired from his job, highlighting the discrimination faced by many at the time. Despite this, the couple continued their advocacy work, becoming enduring symbols of the movement.

Lex Watson was another prominent figure in the early Australian gay rights movement. A co-founder of the Campaign Against Moral Persecution (CAMP), Watson played a vital role in raising public awareness of gay rights issues, challenging discriminatory laws, and fostering a sense of community among LGBTQIA+ individuals.

The 78ers, the participants in the first Mardi Gras parade in 1978, were instrumental in promoting gay rights in Australia. The parade, which began as a protest against the criminalization of homosexuality, faced police brutality, resulting in numerous arrests. This event galvanized the gay community, sparking a more organized and visible fight for equal rights.

Organizations like the Sydney Gay and Lesbian Mardi Gras, the AIDS Council of New South Wales (ACON), and the Victorian AIDS Council (now

Thorne Harbour Health) have also played crucial roles. Their work ranges from hosting cultural events that celebrate the LGBTQIA+ community, to providing crucial health services, to advocating for policy changes related to HIV/AIDS and LGBTQIA+ rights.

More recently, figures like Rodney Croome have been central to the fight for marriage equality in Australia. As the spokesperson for Australian Marriage Equality, Croome was a leading voice in the successful campaign to legalize same-sex marriage.

Transgender activist Norrie May-Welby has been vital in advocating for gender diversity recognition. May-Welby achieved a historic legal victory in 2014 when the High Court of Australia granted them the right to be recognized as gender-neutral.

These activists and many others have shaped Australia's LGBTQIA+ landscape, pushing the country towards greater acceptance, inclusivity, and equality. Their tireless efforts serve as a reminder of the power of individuals and communities to effect change, and their legacy continues to inspire the ongoing fight for LGBTQIA+ rights.

Australian literature, while traditionally heteronormative in its focus, has evolved significantly over the years to include a diverse array of voices and perspectives, including those from the LGBTQIA+

community. Queer representation in Australian literature has grown, showcasing the experiences, struggles, joys, and everyday lives of LGBTQIA+ individuals and playing a crucial role in societal acceptance and understanding.

Among the pioneers of queer literature in Australia is the celebrated poet and author, Dorothy Porter. Known for her dynamic verse novels, Porter often incorporated lesbian themes and characters into her work, providing a much-needed representation in the Australian literary landscape. Her novel, "The Monkey's Mask," a lesbian detective story, became a transnational success, opening up a discourse around lesbian and queer identities.

Another key figure is author and playwright Christos Tsiolkas, best known for his novel "Loaded," which was later adapted into the critically acclaimed film "Head On." Tsiolkas, an openly gay man, creates characters that challenge societal norms and explores themes of sexuality, culture, and identity in his work. His gritty portrayal of queer life offers a refreshing departure from stereotypical narratives.

Novelist and medical doctor Peter Kocan has also offered important contributions to the representation of queer identities in Australian literature. His novel, "Fresh Fields," while not explicitly a queer novel, is noted for its exploration of homosocial relationships and non-heteronormative lifestyles.

Emerging voices in the queer literary scene include authors like Benjamin Law, whose book "The Family Law" humorously and poignantly navigates his experience growing up gay in an Asian-Australian family. The book was later adapted into a successful television series.

Elena Berg, a transgender author, has made significant strides for trans representation with her novel "Transitioning," which depicts the protagonist's journey towards self-acceptance and gender transition. The novel stands out for its authentic and sensitive portrayal of the trans experience.

Australian literature's expanding scope in representing queer lives and experiences is a testament to the evolving societal views on sexuality and gender identity. These works offer not just representation for the LGBTQIA+ community but also provide a broader audience with insights into diverse experiences and narratives, fostering understanding and acceptance. They also underscore the importance of diverse voices in literature, enriching the Australian literary landscape and opening doors for future queer authors and stories.

I n the fabric of Australia's
LGBTQIA+ history, gay bars and
clubs have served as vibrant hubs
for community, culture, and
activism. These establishments have
played a significant role in fostering
a sense of belonging, shaping

community identity, and advocating for social and political change.

In a time when society was less accepting of LGBTQIA+ individuals, gay bars and clubs provided a safe haven for community members to be open about their identity. These spaces offered an environment of acceptance and camaraderie, allowing individuals to socialize freely, express themselves openly, and form relationships without fear of prejudice.

Iconic venues like Sydney's Stonewall Hotel, named after the New York City Stonewall Riots, and the Midnight Shift, along with Melbourne's Poof Doof and The Laird, have played significant roles in shaping Australia's gay community. These venues not only provide entertainment and social opportunities but also help build and maintain a strong sense of community among patrons.

These establishments have also been central to the development of LGBTQIA+ culture. Gay clubs and bars have often been at the forefront of music and fashion trends, and they've provided a platform for drag performances and queer art. For example, the Beresford Sundays in Sydney has become an iconic event for the community, known for its live music and entertainment.

The cultural impact of gay bars and clubs also extends to their role in activism and social change. Many venues have served as meeting places for advocacy groups, hosted fundraisers for causes such as HIV/AIDS research and marriage equality, and served as rallying

points for Pride marches and
protests.

Gay bars and clubs also serve as sites
of collective memory and history for
the LGBTQIA+ community. Many
older establishments have witnessed
the community's highs and lows,
from the jubilation of legal victories
to the heartbreak of the HIV/AIDS
crisis.

Historically, these venues have faced
significant challenges, from police
raids in the 1970s and 1980s to
gentrification pressures and the
advent of online dating in more
recent years. Despite these hurdles,
they have remained resilient and
continue to adapt.

Today, the importance of gay bars
and clubs remains evident. While
the LGBTQIA+ community has made

significant strides in societal acceptance and legal rights, these spaces continue to provide a vital sense of community, culture, and history. As we look forward, the enduring significance of these venues underscores the ongoing need for dedicated spaces where the LGBTQIA+ community can gather, celebrate, and support one another.

The history of gay men serving in the Australian Armed Forces is a complex and often hidden narrative within Australia's military history. It's a story characterized by silent service, clandestine lives, personal bravery, and slowly evolving acceptance.

For many decades, homosexuality was deemed incompatible with military service in Australia. Policies reflecting societal norms and prejudices effectively prohibited openly gay men from serving in the Armed Forces. Those found to be engaging in homosexual acts could face severe penalties, including dismissal, incarceration, or even chemical castration. As a result, many gay servicemen lived dual lives, serving their country while concealing their true identities.

Despite the pervasive atmosphere of homophobia, stories of camaraderie and covert acceptance also emerge from this period. Many gay servicemen found companionship, understanding, and even romance within the ranks. These personal narratives contrast sharply with official military policies, demonstrating the diversity of experiences within the Armed Forces.

The latter part of the 20th century saw gradual changes in societal attitudes and legal norms. The decriminalization of homosexuality in various Australian states from the 1970s to the 1990s marked a turning point, prompting the military to reevaluate its stance.

In November 1992, following years of advocacy and legal challenges, the ban on gay men and lesbians serving in the Australian military was finally lifted. This policy change made Australia one of the first countries in the world to permit openly gay individuals to serve in the Armed Forces.

In 2005, the Australian Defence Force (ADF) extended full benefits to same-sex partners of military personnel, furthering equality within the ranks. In 2013, the Sex Discrimination Amendment (Sexual Orientation, Gender Identity and Intersex Status) Act was passed, offering greater protections for LGBTQIA+ individuals, including those in the military.

Today, the ADF not only allows gay men to serve openly but also actively promotes diversity and inclusion within its ranks. Events like the Sydney Gay and Lesbian Mardi Gras often see participation from uniformed military personnel, including high-ranking officials, a powerful symbol of the progress made.

The history of gay men in the Australian Armed Forces is a testament to the resilience and bravery of those who served their country while battling prejudice and discrimination. It also highlights the military's evolution from a space of exclusion and secrecy to one striving for acceptance and inclusivity. It's a potent reminder of the progress achieved and the ongoing efforts necessary to ensure equality for all who serve.

The intersection of race and sexuality provides a rich, complex, and often underrepresented perspective within Australia's LGBTQIA+ narrative. It offers insights into unique experiences of individuals who navigate dual or multiple identities and confront stereotypes and prejudices that stem from both their racial/ethnic backgrounds and sexual orientation.

Australia is a multicultural society, home to a diverse array of ethnic communities. For LGBTQIA+ individuals from these backgrounds, their experience of identity and acceptance often interweaves with cultural norms, community attitudes, and racial dynamics.

Indigenous LGBTQIA+ Australians, often referred to as Sistergirls and Brotherboys, face unique challenges. Many indigenous cultures have traditional roles and respect for gender-diverse individuals, which colonialism often disrupted. Today, Indigenous LGBTQIA+ individuals often face the challenge of reconciling their sexual and gender identities with their cultural identities. Despite these hurdles, they have been instrumental in enriching Australia's LGBTQIA+ discourse and championing inclusivity within their communities.

The Asian-Australian LGBTQIA+ community provides another compelling perspective. The experience of Asian-Australian LGBTQIA+ individuals is often marked by dual invisibility, both within their ethnic communities, where conversations about sexuality may be taboo, and within the mainstream LGBTQIA+ community, where representation is predominantly white. Voices like author Benjamin Law have been crucial in breaking these stereotypes, offering a more nuanced depiction of the Asian-Australian gay experience.

Migrant and refugee LGBTQIA+ communities in Australia also face unique circumstances. They grapple with challenges such as language barriers, unfamiliarity with Australian laws and LGBTQIA+ support systems, and potential isolation from their cultural communities due to their sexual orientation. Organizations like the Multicultural LGBTIQ+ Support Directory have been pivotal in offering support and resources to these individuals.

Representation and visibility of racially and ethnically diverse LGBTQIA+ Australians in media, politics, and public life play a crucial role in breaking down stereotypes. High-profile individuals like soccer player Andy Brennan, senator Penny Wong, and comedian Joel Kim Booster are challenging stereotypes and contributing to a more inclusive and diverse image of Australia's LGBTQIA+ community.

However, the intersection of race and sexuality in Australia's LGBTQIA+ landscape also highlights the need for greater understanding and inclusivity. The experiences and challenges of racially and ethnically diverse LGBTQIA+ individuals are unique and complex. Recognizing this intersectionality is essential in fostering an environment that respects and celebrates both the racial/ethnic and sexual identities of all individuals. It reinforces the fact that the LGBTQIA+ community is not a monolith but a vibrant tapestry of diverse experiences and identities, all of which contribute to its richness and resilience.

The mental health of the LGBTQIA+ community in Australia is a topic of immense importance, intertwined with the broader narrative of acceptance, discrimination, and resilience. Studies have consistently demonstrated that LGBTQIA+ individuals face a higher risk of mental health issues than their heterosexual counterparts, due to factors such as stigma, discrimination, and social exclusion.

According to the National LGBTI Health Alliance, LGBTQIA+ people aged 16 and over are nearly three times more likely to be diagnosed with depression in their lifetime. Anxiety disorders are also significantly more prevalent within the LGBTQIA+ community. Furthermore, LGBTQIA+ individuals are more likely to self-harm and contemplate suicide. For example, LGBTQIA+ young people aged 16 to 27 are five times more likely to attempt suicide compared to the general population.

These mental health disparities are often rooted in experiences of discrimination, bullying, and rejection. Microaggressions, whether subtle or overt, can significantly impact an individual's mental well-being. It's also important to consider intersectionality here - individuals who belong to multiple marginalized groups, such as people of color or individuals with disabilities within the LGBTQIA+ community, often face compounded stressors that can exacerbate mental health issues.

However, it's essential to remember that these statistics are not indicative of any inherent aspect of being LGBTQIA+. Instead, they are a reflection of societal attitudes and structural inequalities. The high rates of mental health issues within the LGBTQIA+ community signal a need for societal change - for attitudes of acceptance, inclusive policies, and supportive environments to become the norm.

Australia has made significant strides towards inclusivity and acceptance, with changes in law to protect against discrimination and the legalization of same-sex marriage. However, there is still work to be done to improve the mental health of the LGBTQIA+ community. This includes ensuring access to mental health services that are sensitive to the needs and experiences of LGBTQIA+ individuals, providing resources and support for those at risk, and continuing to challenge discriminatory attitudes and behaviours in society at large.

Several organizations and initiatives are doing remarkable work in this area. Beyond Blue, Headspace, and ReachOut offer mental health support for LGBTQIA+ individuals. The National LGBTI Health Alliance advocates for policy and practice change. PFLAG provides support for families and friends, helping to create supportive environments.

Mental health within the Australian LGBTQIA+ community, while a significant concern, is also a testament to the community's resilience and strength. Each individual's journey and experiences contribute to a broader narrative of overcoming adversity, advocating for change, and building a more inclusive and understanding society. The challenge lies in continuing to push for this change and ensuring that every LGBTQIA+ individual feels accepted, supported, and valued for who they are.

Navigating adolescence and young adulthood can be a challenging time for anyone. For queer youth in Australia, these years can be particularly complex, marked by struggles for acceptance, the process of coming out, and the quest for identity. Yet, they're also characterized by resilience, triumphs, and significant contributions to the broader LGBTQIA+ narrative.

Coming to terms with one's sexual orientation or gender identity during adolescence can be difficult, particularly if an individual fears rejection from family, friends, or society. This fear can lead to feelings of isolation and, in some cases, serious mental health issues. In fact, the National LGBTI Health Alliance reports that LGBTI young people aged 16 to 27 are five times more likely to attempt suicide compared to the broader population.

Many queer youth face the challenge of bullying in schools. Safe Schools Coalition Australia, an initiative that aimed to foster safe and inclusive school environments for LGBTQIA+ students, found that 75% of LGBTI students experience some form of homophobic or transphobic bullying. This hostility can negatively impact their academic performance, mental health, and overall well-being.

However, these challenges tell only part of the story. Queer youth in Australia also demonstrate incredible resilience and play a significant role in advancing LGBTQIA+ rights and visibility. Many are at the forefront of advocacy efforts, pushing for inclusive school policies, better mental health resources, and broader societal change. Their stories, voices, and activism are instrumental in creating a more accepting and understanding society.

The rise of LGBTQIA+ youth groups and organizations provides a supportive community for young individuals exploring their identities. Groups like Minus18 offer social events, workshops, and resources that promote inclusivity and provide a sense of belonging. These organizations empower queer youth, helping them recognize that they are not alone and that their identity is something to be celebrated, not concealed.

The triumphs of queer youth in Australia are seen in their growing representation and visibility across multiple platforms. The success of figures like Nevo Zisin, a transgender activist and author, and Georgie Stone, one of the youngest trans individuals to receive hormone treatment in Australia, demonstrate the strength and potential of queer youth. They are not only navigating their personal journeys but also paving the way for future generations of LGBTQIA+ individuals.

The experience of queer youth in Australia, while marked by challenges, is also one of triumph and resilience. It is a narrative of young individuals embracing their identities, standing up for their rights, and shaping a more inclusive future. The supportive networks, visibility, and gradual societal acceptance that are increasing in today's landscape serve as a beacon of hope for the struggles that queer youth face, underscoring the progress made and the continued work to be done.

The story of queer Indigenous Australians is one of dual identities, double marginalization, and resilience in the face of adversity. Also referred to as Sistergirls and Brotherboys, queer Indigenous Australians navigate the intersection of their cultural identity and their sexual and gender identity.

The history and traditional cultures of Aboriginal and Torres Strait Islander peoples encompassed diverse roles and respect for gender-diverse and same-sex-attracted individuals. However, the onset of colonialism often disrupted these traditions and imposed rigid gender binaries and heteronormative values, which continue to impact Indigenous communities today.

Indigenous Australians already face systemic discrimination and socio-economic disadvantages due to a long history of colonization and marginalization. When you add the aspect of being queer to this identity, it leads to what is often referred to as "double discrimination" or "double marginalization". They face discrimination from the broader society due to their Indigenous heritage and often within their communities due to their queer identity.

According to the Australian Human Rights Commission, the double discrimination faced by queer Indigenous Australians can lead to higher rates of mental health disorders, suicide, and self-harm. They are also more likely to experience homelessness and be victims of physical and sexual violence. The ongoing process of 'coming out' can further contribute to these mental health challenges and social marginalization.

However, despite these hardships, queer Indigenous Australians are resilient and have a strong sense of community. They are actively engaged in fighting for their rights, preserving their cultural traditions, and advocating for greater acceptance and visibility within their Indigenous communities and the broader Australian society.

Today, initiatives like the Black Rainbow provide advocacy and support for Aboriginal and Torres Strait Islander LGBTQIA+ people. It creates safe spaces, offers mental health services, and promotes visibility and acceptance. Similarly, the annual Mardi Gras parade in Sydney increasingly features Indigenous queer groups, reflecting the growing recognition and celebration of this community.

The narrative of queer Indigenous Australians serves as a powerful reminder of the intersectionality of oppression and the need to consider all facets of an individual's identity in the fight for equality and justice. Their experience underscores the importance of community, resilience, and advocacy in overcoming systemic barriers and creating a more inclusive society. While progress has been made, there remains much work to be done to fully acknowledge and address the unique struggles faced by this community, and to ensure that their voices are heard and their rights upheld.

Australian media's role in shaping public opinion about homosexuality is multifaceted and impactful. The narrative surrounding homosexuality within the media landscape has evolved significantly over the years, mirroring broader societal changes and influencing perceptions and attitudes.

During the early 20th century, Australian media coverage of homosexuality was largely negative, filled with derogatory language and homophobic stereotypes. Homosexuality was considered a criminal act and a mental illness in various jurisdictions, and media narratives perpetuated this stigma. Sensationalist reporting, scant coverage of LGBTQIA+ rights, and the demonization of queer individuals were unfortunately commonplace. This period saw the rampant pathologizing of homosexuality, leading to harmful stereotypes and fuelling social prejudices.

However, by the 1970s and 80s, during the rise of the gay liberation movement, the narrative began to shift. The media played an essential role in giving voice to the burgeoning movement, providing coverage of protests and rights campaigns. Activist publications such as "Campaign" magazine emerged, offering a platform for LGBTQIA+ individuals and their allies to express their views, challenge discrimination, and foster community.

Yet, the 1980s also marked the arrival of the HIV/AIDS crisis, which significantly impacted public perceptions of homosexuality. Media narratives often stigmatized those with the disease, framing HIV/AIDS as a "gay plague" and further marginalizing the gay community.

Despite this, media also played a part in raising awareness about the disease and the need for funding, research, and de-stigmatization.

With the advent of the 21st century and the growth of digital media, there has been an increasing visibility of LGBTQIA+ individuals and narratives. TV shows like "Please Like Me" and films like "Holding the Man" have brought queer stories to mainstream audiences, humanizing the LGBTQIA+ experience and challenging stereotypes. The marriage equality debate, widely covered in the media, saw a significant shift in public opinion, with media platforms utilized effectively by campaigners to sway public sentiment and political will.

However, media representation is not always positive or accurate.

Media outlets can perpetuate harmful stereotypes, underrepresent certain segments of the LGBTQIA+ community, and focus disproportionately on cisgender gay and lesbian individuals at the expense of other identities. There's a need for more diverse and nuanced representation in media to reflect the broad spectrum of the LGBTQIA+ community.

Social media, in particular, has emerged as a double-edged sword. While it provides a platform for expression, connection, and activism for many LGBTQIA+ individuals, it can also be a source of cyberbullying, harassment, and the spread of discriminatory content.

The Australian media, while not a monolithic entity, plays a pivotal role in shaping societal attitudes towards homosexuality and the broader LGBTQIA¹ community. Through representation, news coverage, and the narratives it chooses to highlight, media can either perpetuate stereotypes and fuel discrimination or challenge prejudices and foster understanding and acceptance. In an era of 'fake news' and media fragmentation, the responsibility to offer accurate, balanced, and respectful coverage is even more crucial. As society continues to evolve, so too must the media's portrayal of homosexuality, progressing towards a more inclusive, diverse, and truthful representation.

As we delve into a queer future in Australia, it's clear that significant strides have been made in the journey towards equality and acceptance. However, the path ahead is still marked by challenges that must be acknowledged, and opportunities that beckon for further progress.

The decriminalization of homosexuality, the introduction of anti-discrimination laws, the recognition of same-sex marriage, and growing representation in the media are all testament to the remarkable progress that has been made. Yet, it's important to remember that the fight for LGBTQIA+ rights and acceptance is far from over.

Discrimination and homophobia still persist within many societal institutions and interpersonal relationships. Studies continue to reveal that LGBTQIA+ individuals face higher rates of mental health issues and suicide than their heterosexual counterparts, indicative of ongoing prejudice and discrimination.

Indigenous queer individuals and queer people of color often experience multiple layers of marginalization due to their intersecting identities. Moreover, transgender and gender-diverse individuals face distinct challenges in terms of legal recognition, healthcare access, and social acceptance. The battle for comprehensive sex education, inclusive of all identities and orientations, remains an ongoing concern.

The good news, however, is that the future is ripe with opportunity for continued progress. Increasingly, young Australians are challenging binary norms and embracing a more fluid understanding of gender and sexuality. Schools and universities are implementing policies to ensure safer and more inclusive environments for queer students.

In the corporate world, more organizations are recognizing the importance of diversity and inclusion, adopting LGBTQIA+ friendly policies, and supporting queer employees. The media continues to play a pivotal role in challenging stereotypes and providing a platform for queer voices and stories.

The rise of digital platforms and social media has provided an avenue for increased visibility, community building, and advocacy. It has allowed for the sharing of diverse stories, has given a voice to those who have been historically marginalized, and has the potential to influence societal perceptions and norms significantly.

Legal and policy reforms are still needed in various areas, such as transgender rights, protection against conversion therapy, and improving healthcare access for LGBTQIA+ individuals. Activism and advocacy remain crucial components of achieving these changes.

The outlook of a queer future in Australia is one that calls for continued efforts to foster a society that not only accepts but celebrates diversity in all its forms. It's a future where each individual's identity is respected and valued, where love is recognized in all its variations, and where rights and opportunities are not determined by one's sexual orientation or gender identity. This vision of the future is not only possible but essential, requiring the collective efforts of all Australians, queer or otherwise. As we move forward, it's the lessons from our history, the challenges of our present, and the hopes for our future that will guide our path towards an inclusive, equitable, and queer-friendly Australia.

In the journey that we have undertaken in "Down Under Gay," we've traced a path through history, culture, struggle, and triumph that is as multifaceted and vibrant as a rainbow - a fitting emblem for the gay community in Australia.

As we navigated the intricate tapestry of experiences, emotions, and events that make up the Australian gay narrative, we encountered moments that stirred our hearts with both joy and sorrow. The strength, resilience, and unyielding spirit of the individuals and communities we encountered have left an indelible mark, underscoring the tenacity of the human spirit.

From the whisper of hidden love in historical times, to the present day's resonant shout of pride and acceptance, the chronicle of gay life in Australia is a testament to how far we've come, and an inspiration to continue the work that remains.

It's essential to remember that the history we explored is not just 'gay' history - it is Australian history, human history. It's a shared narrative that informs the fabric of our society, reminding us of the need for empathy, understanding, and acceptance.

The journey doesn't end with the final page of this book. As long as there are stories to tell, voices to amplify, rights to advocate, and love to celebrate, the journey continues. As readers, as individuals, as part of the global community, our understanding, empathy, and advocacy are invaluable in ensuring that all voices are heard, all identities respected, and all forms of love celebrated.

In this afterword, I extend a heartfelt thank you to all who have made this book possible and to you, dear reader, for accompanying us on this enlightening journey. May it inspire us all to write our own narratives of acceptance, understanding, and love, and may we carry these narratives forward into a world that continues to strive for equality, respect, and understanding for all.

www.ingramcontent.com/pod-product-compliance
Lightning Source LLC
Chambersburg PA
CBHW051349280526
45784CB00007B/2877